54052

W9-BCO-475

DEMCO

OUTDOOR ADVENTURE!
ARCHERY

Adam G. Klein

ABDO
Publishing Company

visit us at
www.abdopublishing.com

Published by ABDO Publishing Company, 8000 West 78th Street, Edina, Minnesota 55439.
Copyright © 2008 by Abdo Consulting Group, Inc. International copyrights reserved in all
countries. No part of this book may be reproduced in any form without written permission from the
publisher. The Checkerboard Library™ is a trademark and logo of ABDO Publishing Company.

Printed in the United States.

Cover Photo: iStockphoto
Interior Photos: Alamy pp. 11, 27; AP Images pp. 14, 20, 25; BillMARCHEL.com p. 23;
       Corbis pp. 9, 22, 29; Getty Images pp. 15, 24; Index Stock p. 5; iStockphoto pp. 1, 13, 15, 21;
       Neil Klinepier pp. 9, 12-13, 16, 17, 18, 19; North Wind p. 7

Series Coordinator: Rochelle Baltzer
Editors: Rochelle Baltzer, Megan M. Gunderson
Art Direction & Cover Design: Neil Klinepier

Library of Congress Cataloging-in-Publication Data

Klein, Adam G., 1976-
 Archery / Adam G. Klein.
    p. cm. -- (Outdoor adventure!)
 Includes index.
 ISBN 978-1-59928-955-7
 1. Archery--Juvenile literature. I. Title.

GV1189.K54 2008
799.32--dc22
                                        2007029163

CONTENTS

4

BEGINNER'S LUCK

Andy drew back his arrow and carefully lined it up with the distant target. With a look of determination, he let the arrow fly. It landed just off center of the bull's-eye. He turned to Megan and proudly said, "You know, archery takes years of practice. People train for hours to perfect their skills."

Megan pulled back her arrow with all her strength. Slowly and steadily, she aimed and released the arrow. It soared toward the target. Bull's-eye! It hit the target square in the center, just millimeters from where her instructor's arrow had sunk. "Years of practice, sure," Megan thought.

"Well, I guess you have beginner's luck," Andy said. Feeling **confident**, Megan drew another arrow from her quiver. She was determined to prove that luck had nothing to do with it.

Worldwide, people of all ages and skill levels enjoy archery.

5

BACK IN TIME

The history of archery goes back thousands of years. The bow and arrow **revolutionized** early hunting methods. It allowed hunters to kill animals from a distance. Before this, people had to get close to an animal to slay it. Ancient Egyptians used the bow and arrow as early as 5000 BC for hunting and combat.

The bow has been the most widely used weapon in recorded history. Ancient Egyptians and Greeks practiced archery for both recreational and military purposes. Over time, other countries began to use and improve the weapon.

In the AD 1500s, European militaries replaced bows with firearms. By the end of the century, people rarely used the bow as a war weapon. Instead, it returned to its use in games and hunting.

Today, archery is often known as a sport of skill. But, many of its basic concepts have remained the same throughout history.

ROBIN HOOD

Archery was a major part of English culture during the Middle Ages. In fact, a royal order in 1363 required all Englishmen to practice the sport on Sundays and holidays.

Robin Hood is a legendary English archer from the Middle Ages. According to stories and ballads, he was a hero for common people. He also became known for his mastery in shooting the bow and arrow.

The mythical Robin Hood is said to have been skilled enough to split an arrow with his own. Today, the term *Robin Hood* is used for this rare shot. When archers shoot *Robin Hoods*, they usually keep the split arrows as trophies.

THE BOW

The three basic types of bows are the longbow, the recurve bow, and the compound bow. The longbow is the oldest of these designs. This bow is slightly curved and usually about six feet (2 m) tall. It can hit a target from about 650 feet (200 m). Few longbows are sold today. But, some archers still enjoy shooting the classic longbow.

As the longbow developed, outward curves were added to its ends for **flexibility**. This new design is called the recurve bow. The curves make the bow easier to shoot. The recurve bow is also called the Olympic bow because it is the only style allowed at the Olympic Games.

In 1966, H.W. Allen created the compound bow. Allen placed a series of **pulleys** at the tips of a bow. The pulleys improved the bow's performance. They made the bowstring easier to draw steadily, which increased the bow's power and **accuracy**.

TODAY, COMPOUND BOWS ARE USED IN COMPETITIVE HUNTING EVENTS.

The compound bow's pulley system makes it easier for an archer to hold an aim for a long amount of time. For this reason, compound bows are especially useful when hunting.

Originally, bows were made of wood. Wood was strong, **flexible**, and widely available. Over time, people added materials such as bone to strengthen the bows. Later, **fiberglass** and plastic also became available for use. These materials make the modern bow more **efficient**.

CHOOSING A BOW

Before purchasing a bow, an archer must determine his or her draw length and draw weight. The distance that a person can draw an arrow is called draw length.

A simple way to measure draw length is to use a yardstick. Have someone extend the yardstick at the top of your chest. Then, stretch out your arms as far as possible on the yardstick. The number on the stick at the end of your fingers is your estimated draw length.

Draw weight is measured by the amount of force needed to draw a bow a specific distance, usually 28 inches (71 cm). That force is measured in pounds.

Beginners and children use bows with a draw weight of 20 pounds (9 kg) or less. Men use 50-pound (23-kg) bows in tournaments, while women use 34-pound (15-kg) bows. Remember that in archery, **accuracy** is more important than strength. Bows with a draw weight of 100 pounds (45 kg) or more are available, but they are not always the best choice.

It is important for an archer to find a bow that fits properly. For a beginner, the lighter the draw weight, the more he or she can focus on proper posture and aim.

THE ARROW

The basic parts of an arrow are the shaft, the cresting, the nock, the head, and the fletching. The shaft is the main body of an arrow. It is made of wood, **fiberglass**, **aluminum**, or carbon. Cresting are the marks on the shaft. Archers use cresting to identify their arrows.

The nock is located at the back end of an arrow. It is notched so it can hook onto a bowstring. The arrowhead is located at the point of an arrow. Arrowheads are made in different sizes and weights.

ARROWHEAD

The fletching is the feathers that are attached to an arrow. These feathers stabilize the arrow as it soars through air. In this way, the fletching helps provide shooting **accuracy**.

TOURNAMENT ARROWS ARE MADE OF ALUMINUM OR CARBON GRAPHITE

The weight of an arrowhead is balanced and stabilized by the fletching. For example, hunting and fishing arrowheads are heavier than target practice arrowheads. So, they require larger feathers to stay balanced during flight. Archers must also pay attention to an arrow's marked spine value. The spine value must be **compatible** with a bow's draw weight. If an

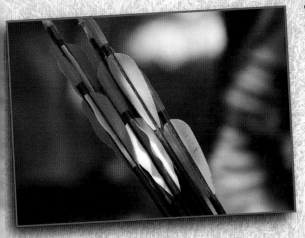

CRESTING

FLETCHING

SHAFT

NOCK

arrow's spine is too weak or too strong, the arrow will not fly straight in the aimed direction. In addition, an arrow should be about 3.75 inches (9.53 cm) longer than its shooter's draw length.

EQUIPMENT

Olympic archers use as many as seven stabilizers on one bow!

SHOULDER QUIVERS ARE IDEAL FOR BOW HUNTERS.

Bow equipment is called tackle. Some tackle is important for protection. Archers wear shooting gloves or finger tabs to keep their hands and fingers from becoming sore. When releasing an arrow, the bowstring can hit the shooter's arm. So, some archers wear arm guards to avoid a painful sting.

Other types of tackle attach to bows. A stabilizer is a small weight that attaches to the bow handle. It projects forward toward the target. When an arrow is released, vibrations run down the shooter's hands and arms. This can affect the arrow's **accuracy**. Stabilizers help absorb these vibrations. Archers use

15

Belt and pocket quivers are used by tournament and field archers.
They are smaller than back and shoulder quivers and hold up to six arrows.

as many stabilizers as they feel comfortable
with. However, beginners should learn archery
basics before using them.

Archers use another type of tackle called a
quiver to protect and store arrows. A quiver is
a leather or plastic tube that can be carried
over the shoulder or hung from a belt. Some
bows have built-in quivers that can hold
four to six arrows. Yet, it is not always
necessary to carry a quiver.

SHOOTING STEPS

When preparing to shoot, archers take a stance. The three basic foot positions are open, even, and closed. Archers choose a particular stance for comfort or power.

Most archers shoot from an open stance. In this stance, the body is slightly turned toward the target. On the line, the back foot is placed slightly above the front. While standing, archers maintain good **posture** but stay relaxed. Once they are comfortable, they nock the arrow.

OPEN STANCE

NOCK

The arrow rests between an archer's pointer and middle fingers. The nock is placed on the bowstring near a mark called the nocking point.

TIP *Before shooting, jog or do jumping jacks for a few minutes to warm up your muscles. Then, stretch slowly and hold each position for at least ten seconds. Repeat each stretch several times.*

The arrow and the bowstring are held with the middle three fingers of one hand. The other hand grips the bow handle. The handle should fit between the thumb and the index finger. Now, an archer is ready to draw.

When drawing an arrow, archers engage their back muscles to push the bow forward. At the same time, the hand holding the arrow moves toward an anchor point. This is the farthest point that an arrow is drawn during aiming. A high anchor point is near the cheek.

LOW ANCHOR POINT

A low anchor point is under the chin.

Archers should use the same anchor point for every draw. By keeping a **consistent** form, it is easier to make small adjustments to improve aim.

AIM

Before aiming, archers must determine their dominant eye. To do this, point your finger at the center of an object across the room. Close your left eye. Is your finger still centered? That means your right eye is dominant. If your finger is centered when your right eye is closed, your left eye is dominant. The dominant eye should be used for aiming.

Trial and error is the simplest way to practice aiming. Some archers use a bow sight to help them aim. This device attaches to a bow about two to five inches (5 to 13 cm) above the arrow. A bow sight has markings for hitting targets at certain distances. Archers use these markings to adjust their aim according to the distance they are shooting.

Most archers aim for 7 to 14 seconds. Then, the arrow is released. As it launches and the bow moves forward, vibrations run through the archer's arm. The archer should comfortably hold his or her position until the arrow has landed.

RELEASE AND HOLD

THE TARGET

Three-dimensional archery is good practice for bow hunters.

Targets are made in various sizes for different courses and competitions. They range in **diameter** from 8 inches (20 cm) to 48 inches (122 cm).

Targets are divided into ten rings. Every set of two rings is a different color. The two rings in the center are yellow. The next two are red, then blue, and then black. The outer two rings are white. One point is scored for the outer ring. Each ring further in is worth an additional point. The center ring, or bull's-eye, is worth ten points.

Three-dimensional (3-D) archery is growing in popularity. Targets for 3-D archery are shaped like animals, such

To an Olympic archer on the course, a bull's-eye looks no bigger than a thumbtack held at arm's length!

as moose, cougars, and skunks. You can even shoot at a target that looks like a dinosaur!

Targets for 3-D archery are placed at unmarked distances. So, archers must guess how far to shoot. Scoring rings represent different parts of an animal's body. Archers earn points based on which part of the target they hit. For example, shooting a heart or a lung is worth more points than shooting a leg or a tail.

OTHER ACTIVITIES

Archery skills can be used for many activities. Hunting with bows and arrows is a popular sport. The minimum practical draw weight for a hunting bow is 40 pounds (18 kg).

Hunters seeking large **game** such as bears, elk, or moose should use a bow with a minimum draw weight of 60 pounds (27 kg).

Archers can also fish with bows and arrows. The minimum draw weight recommended for a fishing bow is 50 pounds (23 kg). Fishing line is attached to the arrow, and a special **barbed** arrowhead is used. When a fish is hit, a small rod extends from the bow. Archers use this rod to reel in their catch. Many kinds of fish can be caught with bows, including large fish such as sharks!

Ski archers carry their bows in special backpacks. Their arrows are stored at shooting locations on the course.

There are also many types of competitions and games for archers. Some sports combine archery with running or cross-country skiing.

In some competitions, archers shoot for distance rather than **accuracy**. This type of game is called flight archery. Flight archers use bows with a draw weight of up to 200 pounds (91 kg) and small, lightweight arrows.

When hunting seasons are over, many bow hunters turn to the sport of bow fishing. Carp is the most popular fish species sought after by bow fishers.

OLYMPIC ARCHERY

Archery **premiered** as an Olympic sport in 1900 at the Paris Olympic Games. The sport was also part of the 1904, 1908, and 1920 Olympic Games.

Back then, there were no organized rules for Olympic archery. Instead, each home country used its

At the 1908 London Olympic Games, Great Britain's Sybil Newall won the gold medal for archery. At 53, she was the oldest woman ever to win an Olympic title in any sport!

own rules. This frustrated people, including the organizers of the Olympics. So after 1920, archery was removed from the Olympic program.

In 1931, representatives from seven countries met in Poland. There, they created a set of **unified** archery competition rules. And, they established an organization

Archery competition is part of the Summer Olympic Games.
Since 1994, the Summer and Winter Games alternate every two years.

called the Fédération Internationale de Tir à l'Arc (FITA). FITA set standard rules for competitive archery. Today, it is in charge of organizing international archery events.

Archery returned as an official gold medal sport in the 1972 Munich Olympic Games. Olympic competition has changed over the years. Today, archers shoot 230 feet (70 m) at bull's-eyes with 4.8-inch (12.2-cm) **diameters**. Teams and individuals representing various countries compete to win gold, silver, and bronze medals.

COMPETITION

   Archers can also compete in many non-Olympic competitions. Indoor archery is a great way for archers to compete and perfect their form. Indoors, archers avoid **terrain** and weather challenges. This makes practicing indoor archery ideal for improving shooting form.

   In the 25-meter (82-ft) indoor Olympic division round, archers shoot 60 arrows at a 60-centimeter (24-in) **diameter** target. Archers shoot 60 arrows at a 40-centimeter (16-in) target in the 18-meter (59-ft) Olympic division round.

   Outdoor archery allows for longer-range shooting. Most U.S. competitions follow a standard format. This format consists of a FITA round followed by an Olympic round.

   During the FITA round, each archer shoots 36 arrows at four different distances. Men shoot at 90, 70, 50, and 30 meters (295, 230, 164, and 98 ft). Women shoot at 70, 60, 50, and 30 meters (230, 197, 164, and 98 ft).

   The Olympic round is an elimination round. Each competitor shoots 18 arrows from 70 meters. The winners advance to the final three 12-arrow matches. The winner of each match advances until a gold medalist is determined.

Field archery is another fun competition. A field archery course resembles hunting grounds. Archers travel through a wooded course with ranges set up on different types of **terrain**. The distances to each target vary and are unmarked. So, archers must guess the distances when shooting at targets.

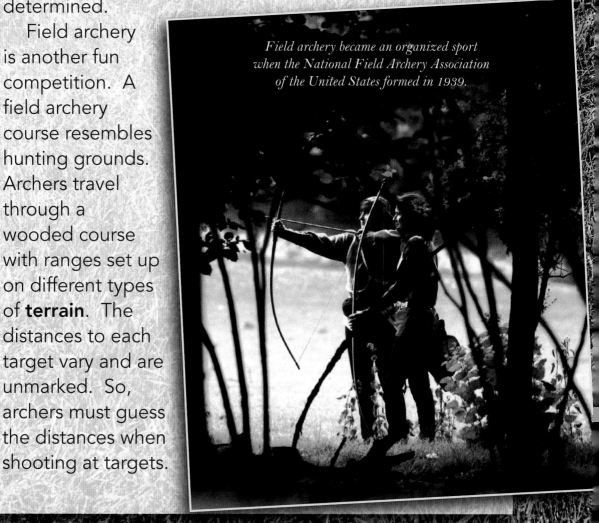

Field archery became an organized sport when the National Field Archery Association of the United States formed in 1939.

ON THE RANGE

Head to an archery range for some fun and exercise! Practicing archery strengthens muscles, especially those in the back and the arms. Certain exercises, such as push-ups, help archers increase their strength.

A range is set up to provide an equal challenge for all competitors. The length of a range varies, depending on the event. The target is at the far end. Behind it is a bale of hay, a dirt mound, or another barrier.

The shooting line is on the opposite end. This is where archers line up to aim. Archers stand in a row on the shooting line and make sure everyone is in line with each other.

Archers remain aware of what is around them and behind their targets. Signals are made on the archery course with whistle blasts. One blast tells archers to begin shooting. Two blasts signals the end of shooting. Three or more blasts alerts archers to stop shooting because of an emergency.

TIP *Wear snug-fitting shirts to avoid interferences with the bowstring. Also, always wear shoes when practicing. Stepping on an unseen arrow lodged in grass can cause an injury.*

Successful archers follow rules so they can enjoy themselves and improve their skills. Be sure that you fully understand archery signals and instructions before setting out on the course. With practice and patience, you can have just as much fun as Andy and Megan did!

Archery improves hand-eye coordination, balance, flexibility, and muscular strength and endurance.

GLOSSARY

accuracy - the state of being free of errors.

aluminum - a light, soft, metallic element that is used in making machinery and other products.

barbed - having barbs. Barbs are sharp projections that extend backward and prevent easy extraction. A fishhook is a common example of an object with a barb.

compatible - able to be used with another device or system without making changes.

confident - to be sure of oneself.

consistent - being unchanging in behavior or beliefs.

diameter - the distance across the middle of an object, such as a circle.

efficient - the ability to produce a desired result without wasting time or energy.

fiberglass - glass in fibrous form used for making various products.

flexible - able to bend or move easily.

game - wild animals hunted for food or sport.

posture - the position of the body whether characteristic or assumed for a special purpose.

premiere - to have a first performance or exhibition.

pulley - a wheel over which a rope or a cable may be pulled to help heavy loads move or change direction.

revolutionize - to change fundamentally or completely.

terrain - the physical features of an area of land. Mountains, rivers, and canyons can all be part of a terrain.

unify - to make or form into one.

WEB SITES

To learn more about archery, visit ABDO Publishing Company on the World Wide Web at www.abdopublishing.com. Web sites about archery are featured on our Book Links page. These links are routinely monitored and updated to provide the most current information available.

INDEX